MY PRIVATE SPA

MY PRIVATE SPA

MARKUS SEBASTIAN BRAUN

BRAUN

CONTENTS

INTRODUCTION

Even as far back as the Harappan civilization, the Mohenjo-Daro settlement in the lower reaches of the Indus Valley (Pakistan) had a sophisticated 4,000-year-old walled canalization system. Some of the houses even boasted private bathrooms, but the heart of this Bronze Age settlement was the "large bath": a 60 x 30-meter site that incorporated a 7 x 12-meter basin. The ancient Egyptians also had private baths, and even shower heads from this era have been found, making it possible to trace the origins of wellness and spas right back to ancient times. Saunas and sweat baths originate from East Asia, from where they spread to Europe and maintain their popularity until today. But also in Ancient Greece sweat and steam baths enjoyed great popularity.

In the 4th century there were around 900 public baths in Ancient Rome, including 11 large thermal baths. A typical example comprised a changing room that offered access to cold and warm baths, sweat or steam baths, with a large warm pool in the middle of the site. These buildings were the center of public life and during the imperial period, they were not only enormously large, but also offered additional functions for play, sports and other luxuries. Furthermore, besides the emperor other wealthy citizens had their own private thermal baths. The bathing culture led to new inventions, such as the precursor to our modern mixer taps with simple lead fittings.

In the early Middle Ages, knowledge of hygiene was lost in Europe and it wasn't until the crusades that the knights rediscovered the ancient bathing culture.

The next generation of thermal baths arose between the 13th and 16th century, and became a focus of social life once more. The number of bathhouses peaked in the early 14th century, before the plague (1348) caused a huge decrease in this practice. The concept of hygiene took on a new level of importance in around 1400, which is why the practice of bathing was revived in the 15th century. The bathhouses also served as banqueting halls where "wedding baths" were celebrated. In the 17th century, water fasts became so popular that even sending jugs of mineral water from certain locations (Vichy, Niederselters) paid off financially. In terms of bodily hygiene, bathing became an ever-rarer practice, but representative baths and private swimming pools were still to be found in castles (Badenburg in Nymphenburg, 1718), and people did bathe communally in "salons" in a mobile bath tub – spas and health resorts served the purpose of entertainment and social contact more than health and hygiene. In 1764, the first bathing facilities were created in Spa in Belgium, and today this name is symbolic of health and well-being.

While the upper class was busy enjoying spas and trips to health resorts, the hygienic situation in the cities was becoming absolutely catastrophic. Public bathing facilities – a public bathing boat on the Seine in Paris was established in 1761 – should offer some relief from this situation since private spas were long in coming. Certain conditions were required before private spas and bathrooms could be introduced, such as a modern water supply system, which was first developed in around 1840. After the gas boiler (1850) and modern "showers" (1870) had been invented, private bathrooms began to appear once more in townhouses from 1900 onwards, although they only became common in the second half of the 20th century, when the number of public saunas began to increase as well.

Initially, private bathrooms were purely functional spaces – compact and often located at the center of a residence with ventilation. The ultimate luxury of the 1960s was a bubble bath with its ever-growing range of scents and colors. It wasn't until the 1980s that bathrooms began to develop as representative spaces, places of relaxation and well-being, sometimes even with a private sauna or a quiet place to sit and relax. Nowadays, private spas are no longer concealed in bathrooms – entire sequences of rooms house extensive wellness areas with their own scents, different levels of humidity and varying temperatures. The Roman thermal baths can now be found in private homes, so why not make them the heart of everyday life.

"Water is the most essential element, both for living and for glorifying life and for everyday use."

Vitruvius – architect, engineer and the most important architectural theorist from Ancient Rome

DE BEAUVOIR COTTAGE

ALL & NXTHING
LONDON, ENGLAND

While designing the new internal layout of this cottage, the bathroom proved the greatest challenge. All & Nxthing were responsible for the whole design while Red Deer architects were entrusted with the planning permissions. To create space for a small upstairs bathroom, the roof at the rear was raised to allow the rear bedroom to be pushed back.

One main aspect was the wish for a big tub and a separate shower which posed a challenge due to the limited space. By cutting the room in half a "wet area" was created, combining the shower and tub instead of separating them. The micro-cement walls that cover the right and rear elevation walls not only add beauty, they also serve a purpose. The material in the wet area is waterproof. All the materials were chosen to create a modern design, while conserving the original character of the cottage.

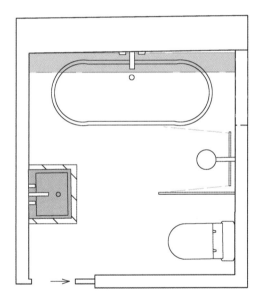

Completion: 2018. *Material:* concrete, brass. *Gross floor area:* 6 m². *Special feature:* wet area.

12

13

15

ALEXANDER BEACH HOUSE

MARK ENGLISH ARCHITECTS
SAUSALITO, CA, USA

This project involved the renovation of an existing single-family home. Perched at the bottom of a hillside, over-hanging the San Francisco Bay in the bayside town of Sausalito, the building is located at a private dock, which was used for the transportation of the required materials.

The renovated space is designed as a dramatic place to share the clients' extensive collection of modern art and mid-century furniture. While exciting in overall form, the original design did not take advantage of the amazing views of San Francisco, Angel Island or Alcatraz. The roof configuration limited the size and location of windows, and the interior walls blocked possible views between spaces and exterior views. The response was to raise facets of the roof to provide immense windows and sliding doors. Careful collaboration with the structural engineer allowed for the extensive opening up of the interior layout, thus creating a fluid impression by using open spaces instead of the typical divided room structure. A spacious bathtub functions as focal element in this context to fuse the master bath and bedroom while offering a unique concept of individual comfort and relaxation.

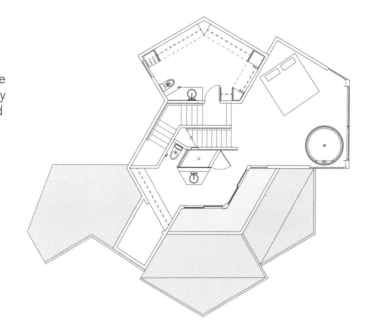

Completion: 2017. *Material:* exposed structural steel, metal windows, engineered oak flooring, LED lighting. *Gross floor area:* 289 m² (loft). *Special feature:* hydronic heating.

18

19

KENSINGTON PARK GARDENS

POWELL TUCK ASSOCIATES
LONDON, ENGLAND

This Victorian house had been unsympathetically adjusted over the years. Powell Tuck Associates' approach was to pare the house back to reveal its original charm: the attractive cornices were restored and the timberwork to the windows and skirtings stripped back to the original Scots pine.

The restoration of the house was completed with contemporary interiors to the bathrooms, bedrooms and kitchen. These modern elements were carefully considered to complement the original house rather than fight against its character. In the master bathroom the cabinetry, bath and shower screens are purposely designed as freestanding elements, allowing the elegant shape of the original room to be clearly read.

Book-matched Statuario marble was used for the walls, floors and basins, while chromed metalwork was selected for the sanitary ware and cabinetry to create a simple, yet luxurious palette. The bathroom is entered via a "secret" door – a fabric-clad pivoting panel which is integrated with the fabric lined walls to the neighboring master bedroom.

Completion: 2013. *Material:* Statuario marble, chromed metalwork, fabric-clad panel. *Gross floor area:* 11.5 m².

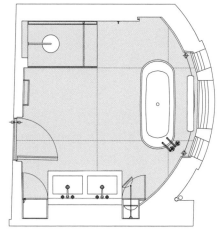

23

SPIDER HOUSE

ITN ARCHITECTS
MELBOURNE, AUSTRALIA

The Spider House is an extension to and renovation of a two-level, mid-century solid brick suburban house that comprised a complete esthetic renewal of the entire house. The project was a collaboration involving the architect, builder and interior designer, who all contributed equally to planning, layout, materials and budget.

This renovation was carried out using a series of infill additions, a new verandah structure, and the reconfiguration of some internal walls. A partial deconstruction of the tiled hip roof led to the creation of a dramatic internal ceiling. The interior palette and materials have been kept simple and consistent and also feature on the exterior of the building, reflecting the outside within. The main materials selected were: cedar ceiling panels, white terrazzo flooring, white walls and brickwork as well as black steel trim and window frames. By keeping the colors and materials simple and natural yet strong, the house does not appear overwhelming and consequently remained distinctive and deliberate in character.

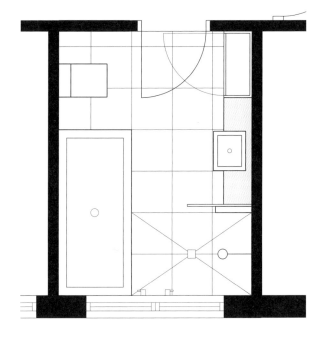

Completion: 2017. *Material:* cedar, terrazzo flooring, brickwork, black steel. *Gross floor area:* 400 m² (house), 9 m² (bathroom). *Special feature:* concealed bath spout, special courtyard lightwell.

BALFOUR PLACE

KHBT
LONDON, ENGLAND

A rundown flat in prestigious Mayfair has been transformed into an inhabitable sculpture. A meandering ribbon becomes an inherent part of all main functions of the newly designed one-bedroom apartment: kitchen, stairs, circulation and bathroom.

The ensuite bathroom is designed to serve as a spa with a purposely separated toilet room which is positioned between master bedroom and kitchen-dining area in order to be also used as a guest toilet. The bathroom, only accessible via the master bedroom, is fitted with a bathtub, a generous shower and a sink. Required level changes become a spatial element to distinguish the entry with a sink for daily use and the area for the personal body treatment. The bathtub, which defines the end of the meandering ribbon, has got a glazed backdrop towards the circulation. It is created for letting daylight into the center of the apartment, allowing views through the space and to highlight the meandering ribbon as a sculptural element. As a distinctive feature and for privacy purposes this glazed backdrop can be switched opaque. The electrochromic glass allows insights whenever it is desired. In essence, the spa is part of the open spatial configuration of the flat with the possibility to separate itself.

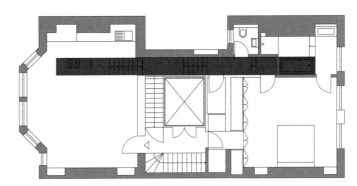

Completion: 2011. *Material:* walnut timber, black and grey tiles.
Gross floor area: 10 m². *Special feature:* electrochromic glass.

26

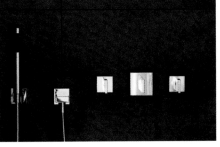

29

SUPER VILLA

CHENG CHUNG DESIGN (HK)
WUHAN, CHINA

Wuhan Greenland Center is a super-tall landmark skyscraper in the city of Wuhan, China. With a height of 636 meters, it was designed by Adrian Smith + Gordon Gill Architecture. This project is located in the center of the Binjiang business district in Wuchang, which will become a super high-rise urban complex, integrating five-star hotels, high-end shopping malls, top-grade office buildings and apartments.

The interior design of Super Villa was finished by Cheng Chung Design (HK). The handling of brightness and openness is a key factor of the interior design. The space sequence created by the design alternates between natural and artificial light. The brightness of space also follows the alternation of natural light and artificial light; transparency, closeness and semi-transparency have been carefully considered and integrated into the process. This interchange is also reflected by the bathroom designs. High-quality materials and contemporary forms determine the layout, which is characterized by a cool, yet classic ambience suitable for contemporary life in a developing urban environment.

Completion: 2018. *Material:* marble, tiles, glass.

32

33

FOCH

JEAN-LOUIS DENIOT
PARIS, FRANCE

This former typical Haussmann mansion has been turned into a three-bedroom apartment for a young family. Gray is the dominant color, giving the ensemble a fresh and elegant impression suitable for a home full of life.

Jean-Louis Deniot and his team may have introduced as many as three or four different gray tones in one room – a paler gray on walls, a darker gray on moldings, and another tone on a door perhaps, so that ultimately the decor is a calmly composed adagio of color, with no dominant tone. And the master bathroom is no exception; determined by the contrast between fine gray gradations and a vibrant painting. By reinterpreting the space, a distinctive and more spacious interior has been evoked. Furniture scooped up in Antwerp, Los Angeles, and hidden corners of Paris gives the rooms energy and a very modern kind of offhand chic.

Completion: 2015. *Material:* marble.

ST VINCENTS PLACE RESIDENCE

B.E ARCHITECTURE
MELBOURNE, AUSTRALIA

As a modern Renaissance home, the St Vincents Place Residence is a new archetype developed through reinterpretation of classical references with a modern sensibility. Positioned behind a significant heritage façade, the new extension is a cultural bridge between historical significance and modern progress. The reworking of older styles in the front section of the original building includes curved cornices, arched doors and custom steel fireplaces, elements that are not typical modern construction methodologies, but feel at ease within the Victorian frontage. Integral to the details is an authentic demonstration of unusual level of craftsmanship, an appreciation of the capacity of mankind. The modern counterpart in the rear extension uses in-situ concrete, terrazzo style stone floors, painted timber ceilings and bluestone walling to create a point of difference from the front.

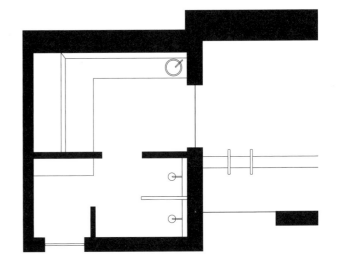

The master bathroom is determined by a mixture of stone and wood creating a classic, yet individual design. A spacious spa area offers possibilities for relaxation where concrete and stone function create a mysterious, almost enchanted surrounding. A refined, casual esthetic is created, incorporating unique vintage pieces sourced from Europe and Asia as direct historic references.

Completion: 2017. *Material:* granite, bluestone.
Gross floor area: 855 m² (house). *Special feature:* underground pool, sauna, onsen.

36

WARRINGTON CRESCENT

RDD ARCHITECTURE
LONDON, ENGLAND

A client eager for space and with a very masculine taste in fashion, cinema and nightlife drove Architect Roberto Di Donato to shape a Victorian flat into an unconventional dark minimal "bachelor pad". Black carpet, dyed ash wood and Marmorino wall finish are constantly playing with lighting and geometry, creating a sequence of glamorous and dramatic impressions.

The apartment does not have a conventional door, the space flows from one room to the other, moving through full-height openings emphasizing the ceiling height. The bathroom area, being the real heart of the flat, is located between the bedroom and a lounge/play space. Conceived as a semi-open space, the basin area is fully visible from bedroom and lounge and forms a connection between the two spaces. The sculptural freestanding basin is exposed under a minimal pendant lamp dropped from the four-meter-high ceiling. When required, visual privacy can be provided with a sliding screen. To fully express and appreciate the ceiling height of the lounge, WC and shower are located inside a lower volume within the room. Inside this volume, the WC is hidden behind a monolithic cabinet and is closable thanks to a folding door concealed inside the wall.

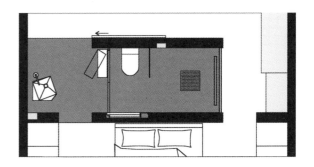

Completion: 2014. *Material:* Oltremateria, Corian, glass, black carpet. *Size:* 98 m² (apartment).
Special feature: open space bathroom.

40

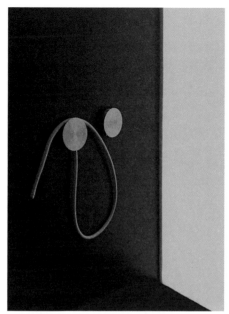

43

PEDERSEN RESIDENCE

BAULHÚS
FLATEYRI, ICELAND

The most challenging aspect of this rebuild was the usage of salvaged building materials, reclaimed lumber and recycled elements. All materials were personally sourced by the architect and scavenged from all over Iceland.

Every single item in the house is vintage, found, reused, or re-purposed and the bathrooms are no exception. The only aim, apart from functionality, was to create a space to be naked, soak and completely unwind. The corner bathtub and sink have been rescued from a busy sidewalk on a main street in Reykjavik. The toilet bowl originates from a WC makeover of Menntaskóli Reykjavikur, the oldest junior college in Iceland. The distinctive seashell chandelier was saved from a personal project in Guadalajara, Mexico; while the wood and glass door originates from St. Josefs hospital in Hafnarfjordur. This approach created a unique project with a high degree of individuality and sustainability.

Completion: in progress. *Material:* wood. *Special feature:* original wooden floor boards.

44

47

DETACHED HOUSE

GEORG DÖRING ARCHITEKTEN BDA
DUSSELDORF, GERMANY

This newly built family home is predominantly cube-shaped and establishes a close connection between outdoor and indoor spaces. The ground floor cube stretches parallel to the street, reaching from one end of the plot to the other. This clearly separates the entrance from the garden. A second cube has been added in a longitudinal direction above this cube, characterized by the front and rear projections over the lower volume.

The ground floor houses the living areas, while the sleeping areas are located on the upper floor. The interior is characterized by the extensive use of exposed concrete for the walls, ceilings and staircases, as well as the wash basins; and the bathroom is no exception. The cubic form of the entire structure is referenced by the strict geometric forms of individual design and installation elements. The surfaces of exposed concrete and walnut provide a demure framework that gives the space a functional, yet individual esthetic. All the built-in furniture, such as the wardrobes, boards, cupboards, dining table, and kitchen furnishings were planned by the architect.

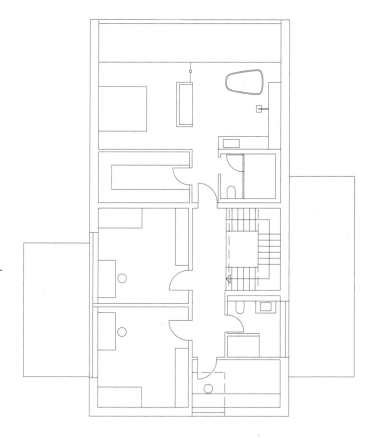

Completion: 2014. *Material:* exposed concrete.
Gross floor area: 351 m² (house).

48

CORCORAN STREET

FORMA DESIGN
WASHINGTON, D.C., USA

These two-time clients engaged Forma Design to completely gut and renovate a three-story row house on Corcoran Street, right off the 14th street corridor, in Washington, D.C.

The lower unit was to become a rental unit, and the upper two floors were to be turned into a modern apartment for the couple. The previous convoluted plan was a series of rooms with a difficult circulation and walls that blocked the light. By opening and reorganizing the layout a spacious, light-filled modern apartment has been created that allows for the display of art and uncluttered living. The design concept throughout the house adapts the idea of less is more. Bright and warm tones for the surfaces interact with distinctive eye-catchers. In the master bathroom, a stone wall made out of different pebbles creates a unique play of natural colors.

Completion: 2017. *Material:* stone floors, natural pebbles. *Gross floor area:* 250 m² (house). *Special feature:* customized clerestory and side lights.

55

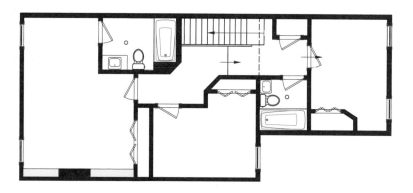

SS
APARTMENT

PAULO MARTINS ARQ&DESIGN
SEVER DO VOUGA, AVEIRO, PORTUGAL

This bathroom was part of a redesign, carried out on the
T1 apartment – a residence of just 46 square meters,
located in the attic of a building from the 1970s and
situated in a privileged area of Sever do Vouga.

The living room originally faced east, with a cozy space
oriented towards the west. The main goal of the redesign
was to swap the location of these two areas, allowing
improved exposure to the sun and better use of the balcony.
A box has been created in the center of the apartment to
separate the living and dining areas from the bedroom. This
box stands out, thanks to the use of a different color, and
also houses the kitchen, bathroom and technical facilities.

Completion: 2014. *Material:* plasterboard, MDF, epoxi
resin, wood. *Gross floor area:* 46 m² (apartment).

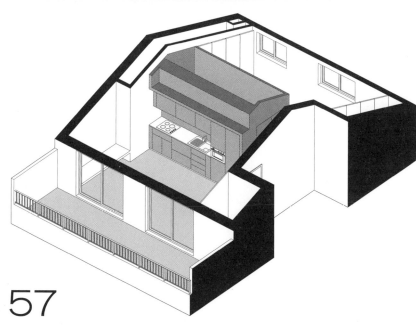

57

PATIOWOHNUNG

WIRTH ARCHITEKTEN
BREMEN, GERMANY

This award-winning apartment has been created using a previously unused basement level. The floor plan has been completely redesigned and the power of the original building made more tangible, with solid walls and ceilings in combination with wooden floors and large windows.

The floor plan has been designed to ensure that all of the routes through the space are circular, with no dead ends. This strategy also helps to reinforce the impression of a large, open space. The bathroom is located where the oil tanks once stood. Instead of trying to artificially simulate sunlight, the space is characterized by dark surfaces. This striking apartment is a modern grotto that amazes with its comfortable and cozy atmosphere.

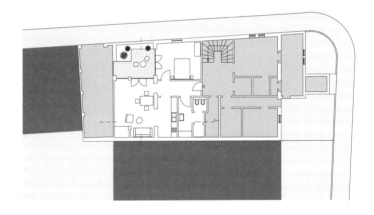

Completion: 2013. *Material:* glass mosaic tiles, floor boards, built-in furniture made of MDF. *Gross floor area:* 71.9 m² (apartment). *Special feature:* shower channel as a simple recess in the creed, without prefabricated parts.

KLEIN
A45

BIG – BJARKE INGELS GROUP
NEW YORK, NY, USA

Klein A45 is the first prototype to be constructed in upstate New York and will be customizable inside and out for future home-owners to purchase and adapt to suit their needs. The tiny house can be built in a period of just four to six months at any location. The design evolves from the traditional A-frame cabin, known for its pitched roof and angled walls which allow for easy rain run-off and simple construction. To maximize the usable floor area, A45 is set on a square base and takes advantage of a twisted roof to raise the tiny home to a soaring four meters height.

A45 is designed to bring the outdoors indoors, with its exposed timber frame in solid pine, Douglas fir floor and customizable space-grade, insulating natural cork walls. The bathroom is made of cedar wood with fixtures by Vola, offering a comfortable environment despite the limited available space. Klein A45 is assembled in modules on site and is built of 100 percent recyclable materials.

Completion: 2018. *Material:* natural cedar, burnt pine, canvas, natural Douglas fir, cork. *Gross floor area:* 17 m² (house).

HOUSE ERG

RALPH GERMANN ARCHITECTES
MONTREUX, SWITZERLAND

The original building from 1911 was stripped back and only the central staircase with its walnut and wrought iron railing was maintained in its original form. All the areas in the apartment have now been joined together, linking the various levels of the space and drawing them together to form a coherent whole. To strengthen the link between the levels, the architect opened the load-bearing walls in the staircase to insert concrete open elements, built on site from molds.

The ground floor houses the living room and the kitchen, connected to the garden. The master bedroom is strategically located at the center of the house and the children's rooms are located on the top floor. The ground floor is large and open, boasting a comfortable multifunctional space. The architect is opposed to single-function space, he prefers open plan spaces with as little furniture and as few doors as possible with discreet built-in cupboards hidden in architectural volumes. Between the big bed that seems to float above a concrete bench, and the open shower, a wood stove also has pride of place. Separated by a thin wooden screen designed by the architect, a bathtub stands in the middle of the room, facing the window with views of the lake and the Alps.

Completion: 2014. *Material:* larch, lime, concrete.
Gross floor area: 240 m² (house).

65

66

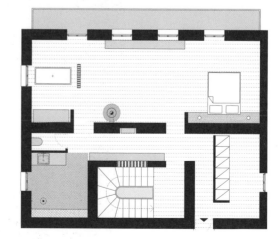

GNATJUKA

REPLUS DESIGN BUREAU
LVIV, UKRAINE

This apartment is located on the top floor of an old
building in the center of Lviv, Ukraine. The bathroom
is characterized by its strikingly minimalist style.

The combination of wooden flooring with bright, modern
surfaces gives the space a sense of breadth, despite it
measuring just four and a half square meters. The walls are
covered with large ceramic tiles and the shower is clad with
small white mosaic tiles. A skylight guarantees a natural
and soft lighting, while two hidden niches offer storage
space, helping to organize the limited room structure.

Completion: 2018. *Material:* mosaic tiles,
laminate. *Gross floor area:* 4.5 m².

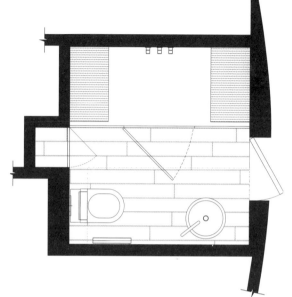

EGG

JONATHAN TUCKEY DESIGN
LONDON, ENGLAND

Egg is a fashion boutique known for its minimalist design approach to the clothes it stocks and the way they are presented to the buyer, acting more like a gallery than a traditional shop. Jonathan Tuckey Design was commissioned to reconfigure the home of the boutique owner, Maureen Doherty, above and adjacent to the store.

A series of timber containers have been inserted into the existing building, dividing domestic and commercial functions and sometimes blending the two. These boxes sit within the volume of the roof and create the nest-like atmosphere of an attic or store room, with skylights allowing light to pour down into the spaces below. Small openings create surprising views through to adjacent rooms and a timber staircase is made up of a series of planks suspended above the hallway. Interior walls remain unadorned and furniture is kept to a minimum, further emphasizing the minimalist esthetic and creating a collection of calm spaces to occupy. Built-in storage hides the clutter of everyday life as they blend into the walls when closed. On the ground floor the project includes a bespoke wooden spa bath supplied by Studio Anna van der Lei set within a bathroom that opens to the mews and that doubles as a meeting room for the Egg team.

Completion: 2015. *Material:* copper taps, ceramic tiles, resin, felt, stained chipboard, painted plaster, timber, brick. *Gross floor area:* 100 m² (house). *Special feature:* timber bath from Anna van der Lei.

74

VILLA ZURICH

GO INTERIORS
ZURICH, SWITZERLAND

Go Interiors was the interior design company commissioned to design the entire interior concept, including this spa, in a villa built by Meier Architekten. The country house-style three-story villa demonstrates both classic and modern elements in the spa area, displaying a striking elegance perfectly suited to this cozy private space. Access to the spa is provided via an entrance area illuminated by a decorative lighting element. This tranquil oasis offers views across the garden and the lake that lies adjacent to the villa. Chains of glass spheres not only serve as a striking decorative element, they also diffract the artificial light.

A tunnel leads into the spa area, where a piece of furniture with a copper basin is located, designed by the client himself. To the right of this, the room opens out to the sauna and wellness shower, and to the left the steam bath and toilets. The rooms are darker in this area and artificial lights have been cleverly integrated to create the perfect atmosphere and make the haptic of the surfaces more tangible.

Completion: 2016. *Project architects:* Meier Architekten.
Material: parquet flooring, different kinds of stone, oil slate stone, copper. *Gross floor area:* 650 m² (villa).

79

81

NEGRITO APARTMENT

RDD ARCHITECTURE
VALENCIA, SPAIN

Located at the heart of the historical center of Valencia, the refurbishment of this apartment aimed to create a comfortable weekend escape for a British couple. The lack of natural light pushed the architect to convert the central patio into a silent connector between spaces. The flat literally revolves around it. There are no internal walls dividing functions, but when privacy is required, almost invisible large wooden screens are used to separate the spaces.

The bathroom moves a step away from the concept of a conventional room. Located on a sort of hallway on one side of the patio, it is designed as a dynamic narration of all the elements of the bathing ceremony. The washbasin is located on a dwarf wall along the passageway in closer proximity to the living room. The same wall creates the separation from the oversized shower area, without the need of any glass screen. The WC area is hidden behind a full-size mirrored door. A freestanding bathtub functions as protagonist of the apartment and is located directly in front of the night area. All elements and wall finishes are made from a neutral colored micro-cement, creating a modest frame to highlight and focus on the marble floor and timber beams of the existing fabric.

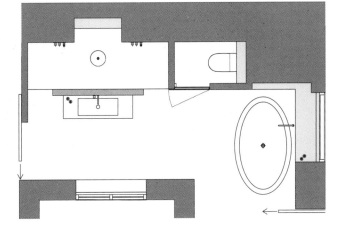

Completion: 2015. *Material:* marble, microcement, oak veneer wood. *Gross floor area:* 110 m². *Special feature:* open space bathroom.

83

VILLA RAPPERSWIL

GO INTERIORS
RAPPERSWIL, SWITZERLAND

A meditative courtyard with a pool and offering views of Lake Zurich forms the core of this villa, built by Kaufmann Architekten. The interior architecture by Go Interiors – who were involved in the project right from the beginning – emphasizes the beauty of the courtyard by blurring the boundaries between the interior and exterior areas. Different atmospheres have been developed throughout the property; such as a stylish and warm guest bathroom and the elegant and generously proportioned master bathroom. A modern training and wellness area boasts direct access to the interior courtyard.

The client has an affinity for technology and this, combined with his demands for highly esthetic rooms that are characterized not only by their functionality, but also their striking sensuality, enrich the interior design. The tailor-made lighting system harmonizes with the modern stylish elements and offers a perfect solution whatever the occasion.

Completion: 2018. *Project architects:* Kaufmann Architekten. *Material:* parquet flooring, different kinds of stone, wood, brass plates, mosaic, handblown glass, Swarovski lead glass. *Gross floor area:* 550 m² (villa).

86

LUXELAKES ECO-CITY FLAT

SHENZHEN QIANXUN DECORATIVE ART AND DESIGN
CHENGDU, CHINA

With the aim of creating a high-quality living environment that integrates aspects of everyday life,
the designer mediated the conflicts between luxury
and elegance and combined the living concepts of
high-income groups with actual daily requirements.

The designer drew inspirations from water and integrated the
colors associated with it into the design. This is reinforced
by the design of the master bathroom, which is characterized by the interplay of bright marble surfaces and golden
elements. The simple colors create an elegant, yet individual
impression interspersed with Chinese design elements.

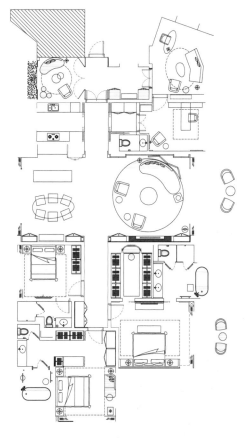

Completion: 2018. *Material:* marble, tile, glass.
Gross floor area: 280 m² (apartment).

94

VILLAGE
TOWNHOUSE

HARRY HEISSMANN INC.
NEW YORK, NY, USA

A key element of this design is a ripple effect that has
been implemented throughout the entire master bedroom
level. The design was inspired by the concentric circles
created when a drop of water hits a larger body of water.
The concept includes a dressing room with large sliding
doors executed in "Verre Eglomise" by artist Miriam Ellner.

In the bathroom, the large shower and WC are located
behind a large wall of hand-stained glass. White onyx
against a blue background is an exclusive eye-catcher and
was the main material used for the floors and walls. All the
fixtures have been specially designed and boast a glossy
finish. The fittings are from the company Dornbracht. The
bathroom can be closed on both sides by floor-to-ceiling
sliding doors that have been let into the walls. Underfloor heating gives the space an extra level of comfort.

Completion: 2013. *Material:* white onyx. *Gross floor area:*
115 m² (whole floor). *Special feature:* underfloor heating.

97

99

A+Z LOFT HOUSE

A+Z DESIGN STUDIO
BUDAPEST, HUNGARY

The architect and production designer Attila F. Kovacs and his wife, art director and stylist Zsuzsa Megyesi, decided that this unusual giant space and movie set-like environment would be ideal for building their perfect home. The HFF knitting factory complex is located in the southern part of Budapest and dates back to 1913–1915. It was originally built as a weapons factory, designed by Arpad Gut and Jenö Gergely. Loft 19, the tower-like 600-square-meter four-story building and the huge factory complex are listed industrial buildings.

A concrete water tank was found in the attic and transformed into a swimming pool. The design of the space is a personal mix of different styles and periods, full of special pieces, collected one by one during decades spent perusing flea markets, auctions and antique shops, or created by the designers themselves. The main features of this striking space are huge windows, much light, the unusual size of rooms and the old structural elements and materials. The original iron doors have been maintained, and the original beams have been reused as book shelves. The bedroom level, in contrast, demonstrates a bold character with a mid-century "boudoir like" atmosphere.

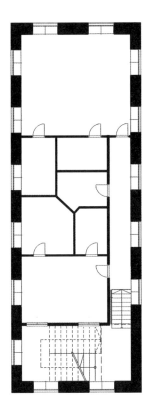 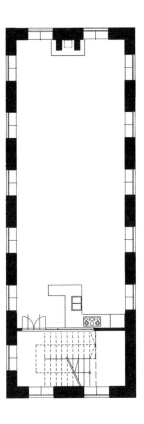

Completion: 2016. *Material:* as found, paint, plaster. *Gross floor area:* 600 m².

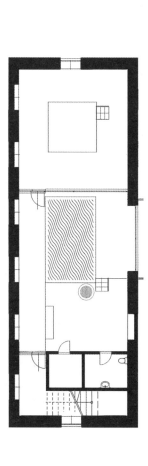

101

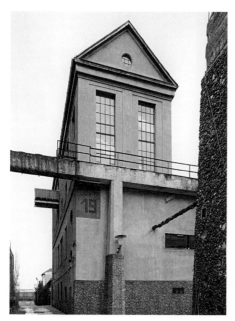

103

AVENUE D'EYLAU

JEAN-LOUIS DENIOT
PARIS, FRANCE

Interior designer and architect Jean-Louis Deniot has replaced the original Hausmann layout of this 270-square-meter apartment, reinterpreting and reinventing the whole ensemble.

When it came to designing the interior, the designer compromised between a timeless style and one evocative of the 1930s. The mixture of noble materials and brown and gray tones creates an elegant impression with a sense of timeless elegance. The design of the master bathroom was inspired by luxury hotels of the 1930s. By using Carrara marble for the surfaces and furniture alike, the whole room seems to be carved from one single block of this precious material. By establishing an elaborate range of contrasts between the materials used and the furniture, the apartment manages to retain its Parisian flair, despite the fact that most of the furniture is not French and all the French 19th-century details have been erased.

Completion: 2011. *Material:* Carrara marble.
Gross floor area: 270 m² (apartment).

SICHIRIGAHAMA HOUSE

SNARK
KAMAKURA, JAPAN

Snark have transformed Sichirigahama House in Kanagawa, Japan, into a stunning beach house. The entire building has a strictly minimalist character and all of the components are white, with a range of different surfaces, or made of glass.

The fixtures and fittings are predominantly light natural colors (wood and leather) or light gray. The façade is entirely closed, except for the entrance to the underground garage and the door. The side of the building facing the Pacific Ocean boasts a number of large openings. The double height of the living room is emphasized by the size of the windows, while the designer chairs give the design a more relaxed ambience. Even the bathrooms are white and minimalist, and the main bathroom also offers striking views of the ocean. A mineral-based, water-repellant plaster has been used to finish the walls and floors, giving the surfaces a waxy appearance.

Completion: 2018. *Material:* waterproof mineral plaster. *Gross floor area:* 488.65 m² (house).

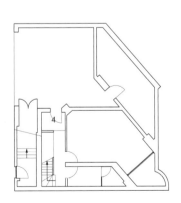  

109

PRIVATE RESIDENCE INDIA

BLOCHER PARTNERS
AHMEDABAD, INDIA

This house in India has been built according to the principles of Vastu – a traditional Indian teaching of architecture that connects humans and the cosmos and is based on 5,000 years of form theory. The office of blocher partners combined this with an insulated concrete construction and intelligent air conditioning technology supported by low-tech natural cooling and shading systems. The living area is a two-story volume with a north-south orientation. This arrangement helps to avoid the interior spaces becoming overheated. The main bedroom boasts a dressing room and ensuite bathroom and is located on the upper floor. Offering sweeping views over the park, this room faces south and is protected by a solid concrete frame. The chosen materials vary in character; both cool and warm tones have been put to good use. Uplights accentuate the surface of the hand-finished sandstone from Rajasthan, the gold tones of which fuse with the cool marble floor.

The interplay between exposed concrete, teak and Jura marble lends the interior a striking elegance and warmth. The long water pool and multi-layered walls both help to passively cool the house.

Completion: 2015. *Material:* exposed concrete, Jura marble, sandstone from Rajasthan, teakwood. *Gross floor area:* 1,800 m² (house).

115

AMBLER ROAD

POWELL TUCK ASSOCIATES
LONDON, ENGLAND

The bathroom and shower room are located in the zinc wedge-shaped extension to the rear of a Victorian terraced house – a contemporary take on the traditional Victorian closet wing. A family bathroom is located at the base of the extension and a smaller shower room in the tapering top.

The bathrooms have narrow slot windows which help to provide internal privacy. Narrow horizontal windows are used to provide privacy and control views out. Fully glazed roof over the shower room allows light in from above and makes the space appear larger. Mirrors are used internally to further enhance the sense of space. The use of bright, brave colors is the key element, not only in the bathrooms but also in the other areas of the renovated house.

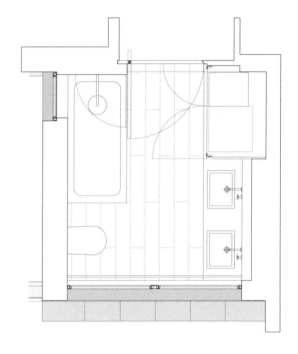

Completion: 2012. *Material:* ceramic tiles. *Gross floor area:* 7.5 m² (family bathroom), 4.7 m² (shower room). *Special feature:* ceramic tiles with high-contrast timber effect print, bright colored doors, narrow windows.

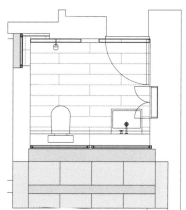

CHALET

BRYAN O'SULLIVAN STUDIO
FRENCH ALPS, FRANCE

Bryan O'Sullivan Studio created this sumptuous Alpine interior for a family ski chalet, comprising living areas, boot rooms, six en-suite bedrooms and indoor spa, all wrapped in a new envelope. The strong façade protects an oasis within, sheltered from the harsh conditions outside. A warm interior of layered textures and tonal timber provides a softened atmosphere in which to enjoy the breathtaking views and relax in a sequence of cozy spaces, with natural, earthy materials and delicate antiques. The bathrooms and powder rooms in the living space are elegant and sumptuous, using fresh whites or dramatic marble completed all with elegant brassware.

Completion: 2017. *Material:* marble, brass.
Gross floor area: 189 m² (house). *Special feature:* hammam, pool, massage room.

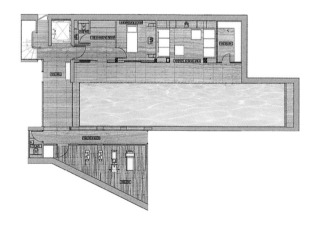

121

3303 WATER STREET

FORMA DESIGN
WASHINGTON, D.C., USA

The clients wished to create a cozy weekend getaway to access Washington's cultural events, restaurants, museums and the Kennedy Center plays and concerts. They approached Forma Design to explore how to exploit the apartment's full potential. The space was tight, therefore a main goal was to create architecture that transformed the space into an open structure suiting the clients' lifestyle and taste.

Stone floors with radiant heat and the latest in lighting and AV technology helped to achieve this goal. A new kitchen and dining area have been added as well as a new double-sided fireplace with TV facing both the living area and the lounge area. The second bedroom became a delightful guest bedroom for the visiting grandkids – with 100 fiber optic lights to mimic a starry sky. The master bedroom suite is equipped with a leather headboard and smoky mirrors that extend the perception of space, while the new master bathroom features a large steam bath/shower transforming this pied-a-terre into a private oasis of relaxation.

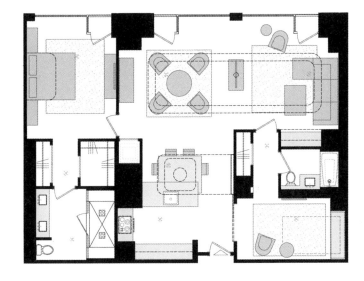

Completion: 2017. *Material:* stone floors and walls.
Gross floor area: 140 m² (house). *Special feature:* radiant heating system for the stone floors.

LITERATURE HOUSE

ITAY FRIEDMAN ARCHITECTS
BERLIN, GERMANY

The client wished to have a space where he could spend his days isolated from day-to-day tasks, allowing him to focus on his affiliation with literature. Rethinking the old functional hierarchy was the first step, which resulted in the reorganization of functions and the electromechanical constructions.

The original bathroom and kitchen were isolated from the main living area by a corridor and a bedroom. To meet the client's requirements, the spatial arrangement has been altered and the bathroom made more compact. The kitchen and living space have been expanded and a corridor was created to gain valuable usable space. The bathroom is characterized by a pattern of green and white tiles. Boasting stone and wood elements, the room appears comfortable and timeless.

Completion: 2017. *Material:* wall tiles, concrete flooring, wood, stone. *Gross floor area:* 57 m² (house). *Special feature:* custom interior design.

126

127

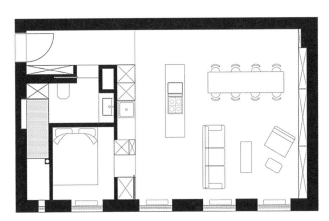

128

120 DAYS PLUS RESIDENCE

SWG STUDIO
HAWTHORN, VICTORIA, AUSTRALIA

The owners of this property are extremely well traveled and have spent a lot of time in hotels. Because of this, they specifically asked that the bathroom should not resemble a hotel bathroom. The narrow L-shaped walk-in wardrobe in the master bedroom forms the link to the ensuite bathroom. The architects chose a natural white color for the walk-in wardrobe fronts on one side and full height mirror fronts on the opposite side to create a larger, more open feeling. This strategy also brightens the space, because the natural light penetrates the door from the ensuite bathroom and reflects off the mirrors.

The walls have been tiled from floor to ceiling with a neu-tral-colored porcelain and dark tiles on the floor to create a comfortable ambience that is not too sterile. The beveled smoked glass mosaic and the bench top of New York marble give the bathroom a rich and luxurious character. The vanity cabinets have been lined with a re-toned timber veneer collection called Siena, which demonstrates a combination of "milk" and "dark" chocolate timber grains running vertically.

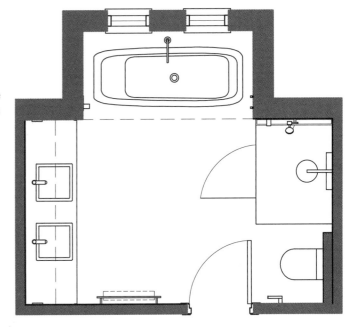

Completion: 2015. *Material:* porcelain tiles, Siena timber veneer, New York marble, beveled smoked glass mosaic. *Gross floor area:* 9.57 m².

131

SSPS APARTMENT

SIEGER DESIGN
SASSENBERG, GERMANY

With this design, sieger design has further developed their Small Size Premium Spa (SSPS) concept as a city apartment with an integrated private spa.

In a washing and shower space of just 3.5 square meters, regenerative applications actively help the users to maintain a healthy lifestyle. Integrated into the open spatial arrangement, the bathroom is located behind a semi-transparent glass wall, which separates it from the living area and lets in daylight. When entering the dry area with its large washbasin, a swing door opens onto the shower area. This can be opened out fully to provide easy access to the wet area with its diverse range of spa functions. In addition to the vertical shower and the rain panel integrated into the ceiling, special massage nozzles stimulate various parts of the body. Electronically controlled water outlets invite you to enjoy automated sequence showers in a seated position. When the spa applications are in use, the separate guest toilet can also be used.

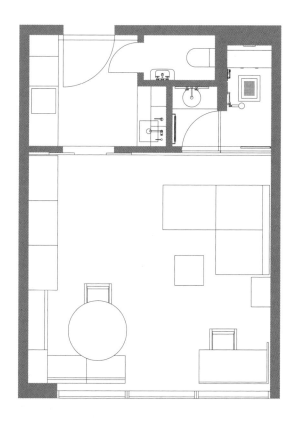

Completion: 2018. *Material:* natural stone, fittings with dark bronze matt finish. *Gross floor area:* 35 m². *Special feature:* rain panel, massage jets, digital control.

SAUNA KÄPYLÄ

PAVE ARCHITECTS
OULU, FINLAND

A striking new sauna building has been added to the courtyard of this 19th-century villa. This contemporary solution fulfills a functional purpose and negates the need for refurbishments on the original villa – thus protecting the valuable heritage of the site. The annex has been placed in close proximity to the shoreline, in place of an old sauna building from the 1960s. With all boxes ticked for the Finnish sauna experience, Sauna Käpylä has its own kitchen, a living room and even a bedroom.

The gable-roofed construction is embedded in the plot, with views from the sauna room opening to the sea through the fully glazed walls on the shore side. Thus, this traditional wooden log sauna functions as an architectural link between the characteristic features of traditional Finnish architecture and an innovative approach to creating a contemporary living environment that interacts with the surrounding landscape.

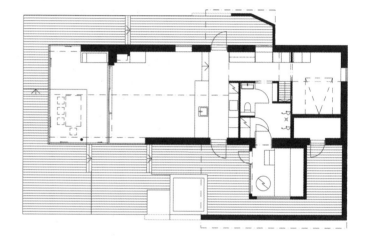

Completion: 2017. *Material:* concrete, pine and larch wood, log. *Gross floor area:* 117 m².

138

APARTMENT S

IFUB*
VIENNA, AUSTRIA

This project shows a very different side of living in Austria's capital city. The house itself – an Art Deco mansion built in 1931 – consists of three separate apartments. The lowest raised ground floor apartment was occupied by the clients in 2013. Besides the details found in the apartment itself, childhood memories and the client's strong personal connection to the place, the design also needed to incorporate other conversions carried out over the decades. Interventions were therefore done very cautiously and the floor plan underwent only minimal changes.

The "big" bath is still relatively small as the original dimensions have not been changed, but improved organization, plus a wall covered by a mirror cabinet make the room feel much bigger. A special detail of the design is the existing door into the library, which was retained at the request of the clients but is now a hidden door in the left mirror cabinet. The design follows the same principles as the kitchen and the shower bath. Modest surfaces in combination with black steel frames give the room order and clarity. The clean look is intensified by the dark terrazzo floor.

Completion: 2015. *Material:* black steel, dark terrazzo flooring. *Gross floor area:* 205 m² (apartment).

J N HOUSE WITH POOLHOUSE

JACOBSEN ARQUITETURA
RIO DE JANEIRO, BRASIL

In the mountains of Petrópolis, an hour and a half from Rio de Janeiro, this property was chosen by a Carioca couple as a place to spend their weekends in the company of family and friends. Despite its size, this house has the aura of a hiding place, a cozy retreat hidden from civilization by the mountains and forests.

The main house forms the core of the property, with a swimming pool and a spa on one side. A little further away are the tennis courts and leisure pavilion, with the maid's quarters beyond. Wood is the dominating material used for the main volumes, while irregular boulders help to embed the ensemble into the surrounding nature. The construction system was designed as the result of a complex research process using highly specialized calculations. This not only creates a new esthetic, it also transforms architectural elements into structural components. The wooden parts were designed in the form of porticos: the vertical slats provide privacy and thermal comfort, while the horizontal ones cover the rooms. The house creates different atmospheres with varying degrees of brightness. During the day, the porticoes create a fascinating play of light and shadows and by night the lights give the rooms their cozy character.

Completion: 2011. *Material:* pine, white granite, Indonesian green stone, Brazilian teak. *Gross floor area:* 2,744 m² (house).

146

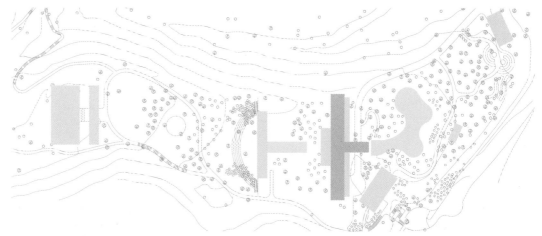

147

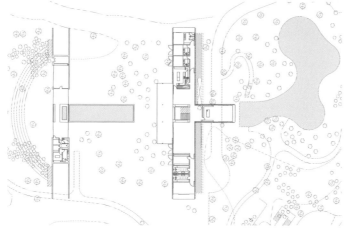

NO 13 HOUSE

OFFICE ISTANBUL ARCHITECTS
ISTANBUL, TURKEY

This refurbishment of a 1990s building has created a new residence for a young couple. The renovated space stretches across three stories, offering comfortable living areas, a working area, a cinema room and two guest bedrooms.

The bathrooms and stairs have been equipped with anti-slip marble flooring. The master bathroom is spacious and boasts a bath tub and a long basin for two people. For daily life, a small shower has been added on the same floor, located near the walk-in closet. The guest bathroom located on the separate guest floor is designed as a compact shower area with anti-slip marble slabs and a small cube-shaped basin. A small restroom has been added to the ground floor. Black oak veneer surrounds the cloak room and restroom, creating the impression of a black box. All of the bathroom elements are determined by a simple and minimal formal language, combined with high-quality materials that create an exciting mixture of functional and luxurious esthetics.

Completion: 2015. *Material:* marble, natural and black oak veneer, brushed oak, glass. *Gross floor area:* 210 m² (house).

150

151

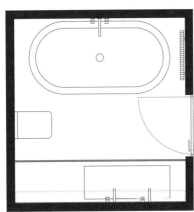

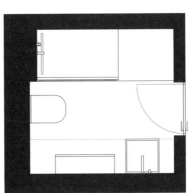

152

SINGEL RESIDENCE

129 INTERIOR ARCHITECTS
AMSTERDAM, THE NETHERLANDS

This residence at the Singel, Amsterdam, is a conglomeration of several functions housed in freestanding volumes. The kitchen and wardrobe are located near the entrance and have been combined into one single volume.

The bath and bedroom is hidden in a volume at the back of the house. Seen from the open living area, a key focus of the design is a dense vertical garden along one wall that continues all the way to the roof terrace. This strikingly lush wall forms a dynamic contrast to the glossy white surfaces of the furnishings. The design is minimalist yet modern, offering residents a luxurious setting that meets all the needs of daily life.

Completion: 2010. *Material:* aluminum, burl walnut wood, epoxy, glass, plant wall. *Gross floor area:* 140 m². *Special feature:* panorama view.

154

155

PENTHOUSE NIEDENAU

SCHMIDT HOLZINGER INNENARCHITEKTEN
FRANKFURT/MAIN, GERMANY

The floors and walls have been fitted with a join-free damp-proof surface. The concrete gray of this surface gives the room the modern character the owners desired. The light sheen of the surfaces transports daylight from the large windows deep into the room.

A large freestanding bathtub is located in front of the window, ensuring imposing views of the high-rise towers. The wall at the entrance to the shower is covered with a natural stone mosaic. The surface of each mosaic tile has been sanded at a slight angle, which gives the wall a raw pixelated texture. A plane glass panel separates the shower from the room. The wash basin of Mutenye wood has a honey-tone color, which gives the room a more comfortable and cozier atmosphere, contrasting the cool gray tones. This warm tone is repeated in the light fixture on the mirror.

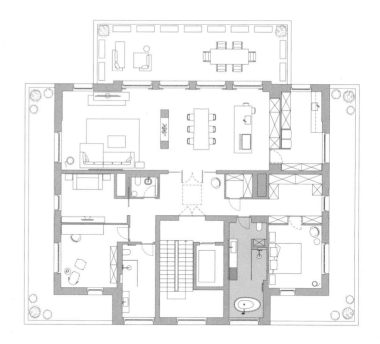

Completion: 2017. *Material:* Marmorino Veneziano, natural stone mosaique, Mutenye wood. *Gross floor area:* 260 m² (house), 16 m² (bathroom). *Special feature:* frameless shower enclosure, joint-free coating.

BRONTE HOUSE

ROLF OCKERT. ARCHITECT.
SYDNEY, AUSTRALIA

The clients approached Rolf Ockert. Architect. and asked him to created a home that would give them the feeling of being on holiday, every day. Although the view was fantastic, the site was very small and suffocated by overbearing neighboring dwellings. The finished house, though, feels generous and as if it is alone with the ocean and the sky.

A rich but reduced palette of strong, earthy materials, such as concrete walls, timber flooring and ceilings, rust metal finishes and thick, textured renders, contrasts with the fine detailing of the interior and anchors the residence against the airy, light aspect created by the opening to the views. The bathrooms are designed as a mixture of elegance and comfort completed by high-quality materials. Single elements like oriental and Asian-inspired accessories complete the atmospheric and individual approach.

Completion: 2012. *Material:* marble floor tiles, glass mosaic wall tiles, walnut cabinetry. *Gross floor area:* 310 m² (house).

162

163

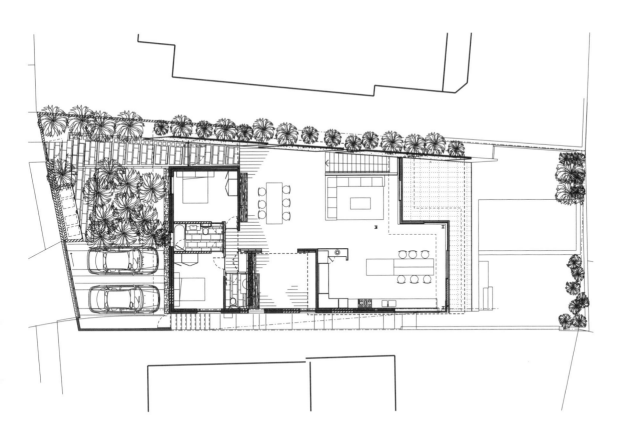

165

CASCADING CREEK HOUSE

BERCY CHEN STUDIO
AUSTIN, TX, USA

Cascading Creek House was conceived as an extension and outgrowth of the limestone and aquifers of the Central Texas geography. The roof structure is configured to create a natural basin for the collection of rainwater, not unlike the vernal pools in the outcroppings of Enchanted Rock, a state park located outside of Austin, Texas. The primary formal gesture of the project inserts two long native limestone walls into the site. The siting of the boundary walls and building elements was informed by the preservation of three mature native oaks. The walls are the boundary between domesticated and native: naturalized vegetation outside these walls and lush and tropical landscapes within. The program of the residence is configured along the stone walls each of which serves as the spine for the public and private wings, respectively. The offset between the main wings establish an exterior courtyard which serves as an extended living space for much of the year.

Various water features throughout the home and property help create a tranquil spa-like atmosphere. In some instances, they also double as sustainability features as they act as catchment systems for the water collected on site.

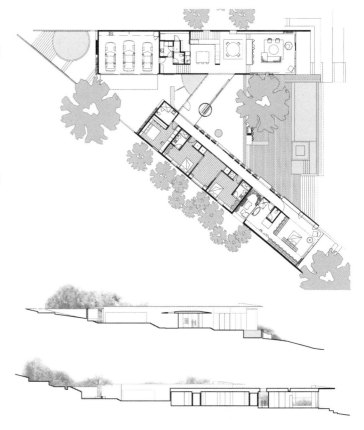

Completion: 2011. *Material:* limestone, wood. *Gross floor area:* 520 m². *Special feature:* extensive climate conditioning system using sun and rain.

166

169

MOSMAN HOUSE

ROLF OCKERT. ARCHITECT.
SYDNEY, AUSTRALIA

This home was designed as an architectural experience from beginning to end. Conceived as two pavilions arranged on each side of a central courtyard, the architecture of the house has been carefully sculpted to take full advantage of the light and views, with side and corner windows which frame landscape elements and add a light quality to the otherwise solid structure.

The master bathroom is characterized by the contrast of warm wood cladding and black and white surfaces. The spacious tub is a sculptural eye-catcher, accompanied by a sauna and a steam room – the perfect place to relax. The dark walls create an atmospheric impression and transform the bathroom into a private oasis suitable for a comfortable family life.

Completion: 2017. *Material:* ceramic wall tiles, black marble wall slabs, dolomite floor tiles, American walnut cabinets. *Gross floor area:* 740 m² (house). *Special feature:* sauna, steam room.

171

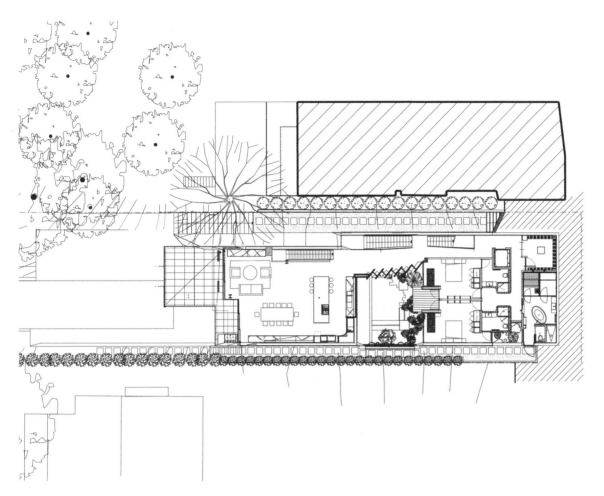

173

SUSSEX STREET HOUSE

MOUNTFORD ARCHITECTS
MAYLANDS, AUSTRALIA

With Sussex Street House Mountford Architects
created an efficient and yet cunning design that
makes the most of light and space on a small living
block located in Maylands, Western Australia.

The steel and timber-framed project employed construction
techniques to provide open-plan living over two levels. The
upstairs bedroom, bathroom and study have deliberately
been designed to take advantage of the views of the trees
on the block while a downstairs bedroom and bathroom have
been designed with the owner's eventual ageing in mind.
For both bathrooms the focus was laid on simple, but yet
expressive features. Bright surfaces, wood and stone melt
to establish a pragmatic but yet timelessly elegant design.

Completion: 2015. *Material:* wood. *Gross
floor area:* 160 m² (house).

174

BODYPUZZLE

HERI&SALLI
VIENNA, AUSTRIA

Alternating fragmented mirror surfaces and lighting fixtures form the basis of this bathroom design. The individual room sections are subtly referenced. The design concept was inspired by the perfection of the human body, which can be also be individually designed.

The mirrors create fragmented reflections of the body – which is also illuminated and staged in fragments by the carefully designed lighting concept. Different sections of the body become visible as one walks past the mirrors. Various tools and utensils for hygienic and esthetic purposes are located behind and around the mirrors. It is in the most private and hidden spaces that the user is finally exposed to the ideal image of the human body. The fragments function as a highly stylized image, just parts of the whole picture. Bodypuzzle becomes a visual reflection of our fragmented society.

Completion: 2012. *Material:* casting technique Pandomo. *Gross floor area:* 11 m².

179

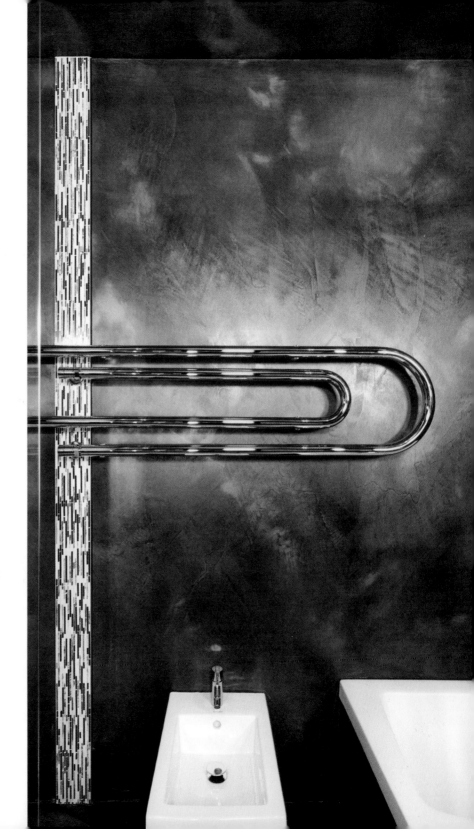

ARROWHEAD

HUGH JEFFERSON RANDOLPH ARCHITECTS
AUSTIN, TX, USA

An existing, nondescript 1960s ranch home on a double lot with a wooded ravine provided the basis for the project. The collaborative team included a very creative client, a design-based contractor, and Hugh Jefferson Randolph Architects. The program added a separate master suite, new kitchen, open living space, and screened porch as well as the development of the outdoor spaces. Material craft and finishes were essential. The team focused on detail in order to give special character to the home while keeping the massing and public image non-assuming. Varied ceiling heights, low and high, and varied finishes, textured and sleek, give the Arrowhead spaces an eclectic impression.

Custom finishes and details, such as the concrete counter with integral sink and Moroccan tile, are combined to create an individual ambience for the master bathroom. A glazed black penny tile provides a dramatic backdrop for an antique tub. Big windows reinforce the connection to the surrounding landscape and the natural light functions as dynamic contrast to the dark interior.

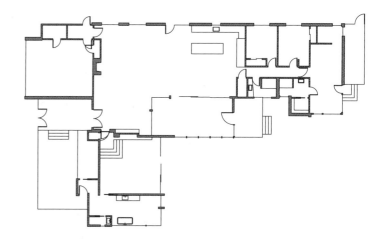

Completion: 2015. *Material:* concrete, stained wood, penny tile, Moroccan tile, painted brick, painted exposed wood beams. *Gross floor area:* 287 m² (house). *Special feature:* custom finishes.

183

185

BEETHOVEN STRASSE

SCHMIDT HOLZINGER INNENARCHITEKTEN
FRANKFURT/MAIN, GERMANY

In this bathroom, fine Portuguese natural stone provides an elegant frame for the few stylish elements. The owner expressed a wish for a large, freestanding bathtub and this was implemented with an organic form in matte white. A freestanding tap is located next to the bath, characterized by its flowing, filigree form. The showerhead and pipe are integrated into a piece of furniture – a combined chimney and cupboard. This unique piece has been incorporated into the supporting wall between the master bathroom and bedroom. The window behind the bathtub becomes opaque at the touch of a button, ensuring the necessary privacy without isolating the room from the outside environment. Two freestanding basins are positioned opposite the large bathtub. No plumbing details are visible, except for the two freestanding taps.

The water flow is controlled via sensors integrated into the floor. A large walk-in shower has been added at the back of the bathroom, this is separated from the rest of the room by a frameless glass panel.

Completion: 2017. *Material:* Portuguese natural stone, burnished brass. *Gross floor area:* 300 m² (house), 18 m² (bathroom). *Special feature:* privacy glazing, non-touch fittings.

189

ST JAMES'S PARK

TG-STUDIO
LONDON, ENGLAND

The master bathroom of this reimagined 1970s apartment in central London pays homage to the luxurious baths in Bath, Somerset. The L-shape of the room has been separated into two volumes, the main part of the bathroom accommodating the large walk-in shower and toilet, as well as a recess housing the double vanity unit. All walls and floors have been tiled with rare Portland stone which was used in Bath and Regent Streets of London. The recess side walls and ceiling are covered in green back-painted glass which is backlit and creates a sense of comfort and calmness.

Clean lines flow throughout the bathroom, with concealed storage behind the mirrors and fittings from the American supplier Waterworks, providing a timeless luxury. A slab of Grigio Billiemi marble imported from Italy completes the impression of timeless elegance.

Completion: 2017. *Material:* Portland stone, oiled oak, gray veined marble, green glass. *Gross floor area:* 9 m². *Special feature:* mirror back wall with hidden storage.

191

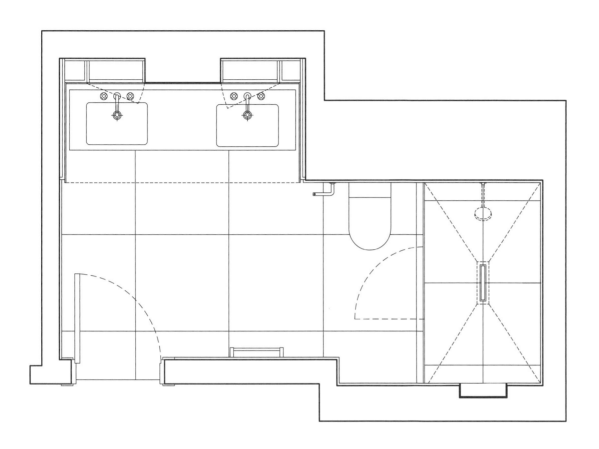

WESTVIEW

HUGH JEFFERSON RANDOLPH ARCHITECTS
AUSTIN, TX, USA

A total renovation and small addition to a 1960s home, this project was inspired by the client's desire to have a house that reflected her personality and lifestyle. Key goals were to create a serene environment with abundant natural light and established connections to the natural setting. Another priority was the balance of open flowing spaces with more private rooms.

The bathroom is characterized by its serenity and lightness. An open shower situated behind the lavatory boasts a teak floor that provides continuity with the room. The spacious openings allow for natural light to flood in, while high-quality materials provide a balance to the clean and simple lines of this contemporary home.

Completion: 2013. *Material:* teak flooring, marble tile, shiplap siding, cut stone. *Gross floor area:* 204 m² (house). *Special feature:* painting by Roi James, open shower.

194

APARTMENT IN XINTIANDI

DLARCHITECTURE
SHANGHAI, CHINA

This master bathroom was redesigned for an elegant apartment in the district of Xintiandi, Shanghai. As the original bathroom area could not be enlarged, the limited space was one of the biggest challenges.

The client required a comfortable and elegant bathroom, thus marble and black iron were chosen as the main materials. Neutral colors function as a modest background. The bathroom is long and narrow and has therefore been divided into three parts. The central one, right in front of the door, boasts a long marble top and two sinks, the WC area in the left corner, and the wet area including the shower and the bathtub. The latter has been separated from the rest of the bathroom with a glass façade and a glass door. The sink cabinet is customized with a white marble top and cabinet doors with a black iron finish frame and mirror in the center. The mirror on top of the sinks features the same frame as the cabinet doors.

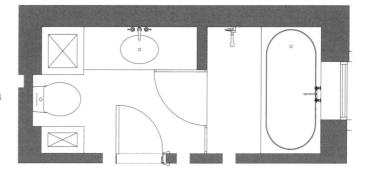

Completion: 2016. *Material:* white and brown marble, black iron, glass. *Gross floor area:* 8 m².

BREDENEY HOUSE

ALEXANDER BRENNER ARCHITEKTEN
ESSEN, GERMANY

With this villa in Essen, Alexander Brenner Architekten were – like with all their residential projects – not only involved as architects, they also planned the gardens and exterior areas and designed the entire interior, including the individually fitted furnishings.

A four-meter-high entrance hall connects two wings of the same height, which stretch out at right angles to the entrance area. To the right are the living and dining areas, with an open kitchen; and to the left the private rooms, which are located on two levels of normal room height. The sloping site also accommodates the children's rooms and guest rooms with access to the garden, with the parents' rooms located above. The main bathroom is located in the most private area, at the end of the wing. This opens out towards the garden with a floor-to-ceiling window tucked behind a recessed balcony. It is not possible to see into the bathroom from outside, but curtains have been fitted for use if required. The spa and sauna are located opposite. The main materials used include Jura Travertine and oak wood. These have been used alternately as wall cladding or furnishing elements, they are also used as flooring in places, creating a dynamic play of different surfaces.

Completion: 2015. *Material:* lime plaster, mineral paint, oak parquet, Jurassic travertine, basalt. *Gross floor area:* 724 m².

CASA BGS

ALVARO MORAGREGA / ARQUITECTO
TAPALPA, MEXICO

Casa BGS consists of two small cabins connected by a living area in the middle of the Tapalpa forest. Each cabin consists of a simple two-story stone building with several openings. The stone composition is demarcated with Douglas fir framing each door and window, resulting in a pattern reminiscent of Mondrian's simplest paintings.

The bath is conceived as a space to be inhabited instead of just being utilitarian. The black granite floor contrasts the metallic bathtub. The shower is located outside the stone cabin within a wooden enclosure and topped by a glass skylight that allows for a view of the surrounding pine forest. The whole bath area is enclosed in wood, including the ceiling which consists of two layers functioning as support of the hardwood floor of the second sleeping area. The lighting design comprises direct installations above the wooden surfaces, as well as chandeliers made of hanging fabric cables. All the plumbing is exposed in copper and bronze to express a sense of sculptural quality.

Completion: 2018. *Material:* black granite, wood, copper, bronze. *Gross floor area:* 185 m² (house).

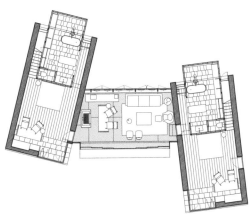

SIMPRUG RESIDENCE

HELLOEMBRYO
JAKARTA, INDONESIA

The clients regularly host parties at home, so they wanted to be able to accommodate as many people as possible in the living room. The built-in furniture has been kept to a minimum, but it nevertheless offers enough storage space. A further requirement was a walk-in closet in the bedroom.

The adjoining walls between the living room and the dining room and the dining room and the kitchen have been removed, creating a new spatial configuration that encourages interaction between these spaces. Tearing down the wall between the master bedroom and the adjoining bedroom permitted the creation of a walk-in closet. The bathroom is determined by marble surfaces and dark wooden elements.

Completion: 2016. *Material:* marble, timber, laminate. *Gross floor area:* 170 m² (house).

214

ARMADALE RESIDENCE

B.E ARCHITECTURE
ARMADALE, MELBOURNE, AUSTRALIA

The overall impression of this three-story residence is lightness – almost an ethereal floating quality created by the sun refracting over the granite façade. Within the lightly colored granite structure, the interiors of Armadale Residence have an unmistakable sense of fun that directly reflects the clients' personalities. The main living area has an eclectic mix of furnishings, combining classic designer items, vintage finds and custom-made pieces.

The master ensuite is a luxurious private space, where the use of granite comes into the custom-made solid granite bath and basins, products developed by B.E Architecture. The clear formal language expresses a sense of classical elegance, while the warm tones of wood surfaces function as a visual antithesis. The bedroom and ensuite bathroom both open onto an internal courtyard planted with Japanese maples. Tucked below the trees is a discrete outdoor shower, an unusual amenity for the upper level of an inner-city dwelling.

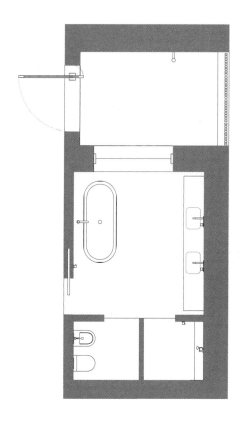

Completion: 2017. *Material:* granite. *Gross floor area:* 550 m² (house). *Special feature:* outdoor shower.

217

INDEX

IMAGE INDEX

223

IMPRINT

The Deutsche Nationalbibliothek lists this publication in the Deutsche Nationalbibliografie; detailed bibliographic data are available on the Internet at http://dnb.dnb.de

ISBN 978-3-03768-245-6
© 2019 by Braun Publishing AG
www.braun-publishing.ch

1st edition 2019

Editor
Chris van Uffelen

Editorial staff and layout
Julia Heinemann, Lisa Rogers

Graphic concept
Johannes Rinkenburger

Reproduction
Bild1Druck GmbH, Berlin